YOU
ALREADY
KNOW
THIS

Original
Inspiration
P U B L I S H I N G

OriginalInspirationPublishing.com

YOU *ALREADY* KNOW THIS

Heather M. Clarke

Original Inspiration
PUBLISHING

ISBN 978-0-9988038-0-7

Published by Original Inspiration Publishing
Arizona, USA

I dedicate this book to my two sons, Tim and Dan, and my five grandchildren, Anthony, Misti, Vivian, Simon and Jesse, and my great-granddaughter, Chloe. Over the years they have all won Best Supporting Actor awards for exquisitely playing their parts in the continuing saga of my life. Well done, you guys!

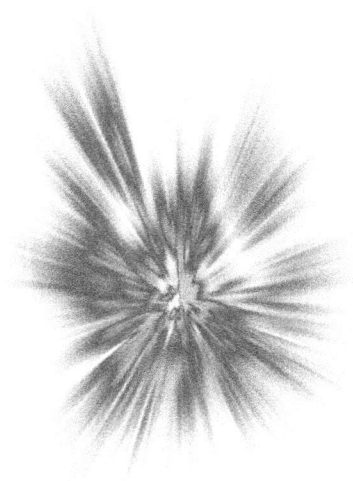

"In *You Already Know This,* Heather M. Clarke, simply sharing through a series of stories and experiences, offers a collection of spiritual gems helping you to awaken to the power of who you are as a spiritual being. Utilizing messages from her guides, common sense and even humor, Heather offers practical suggestions for addressing human issues and challenges through the more expanded lens of your spirit/soul's perspective. This is a book that can be read over and over again. I've used it like a divination tool, just opening to a page to see what I most need to know or remember in that moment."

–Catherine Ann Clemett, author of *Soulweaving, Return to the Heart of the Mother* and co-author of *Anna, the Voice of the Magdalenes* and *Twin Flame Union, the Ascension of St. Germain and Portia* with Claire Heartsong

"A totally delightful read from a dear friend whose spiritual journey can best be described as a devoted and noble pursuit."

– Rev. Hal S. Lafler, D.D.

"This is a peek at the way Heather lives her life in alignment with her guides. An inspiration for living an intentional life."

–Mary Canady, Chief Operating Officer, Arizona Enlightenment Center

ACKNOWLEDGMENTS

I have been blessed to have a lot of moral support with this project. Elmas Vincent is the best "idea guy" I have ever worked with. I have known him for years, and every time I needed a title for something or some marketing advice, I would meet him somewhere for an hour or so and come away with pages of ideas to finish whatever project I was working on.

I knew I was going to need some help with the cover design and the layout of the book, and I was getting ready to tackle it on my own when I remembered our son Tim does this for a living! Geez! He graciously volunteered to help me fine-tune it as the need arose. My freelance designer, Cassandria De Bellefeuille, helped the whole project come together when it was time to go to press by creating the basic design elements of the cover and handling the interior layout. She and Tim made it all seem so easy! I also thank Sandy Burke, Trish Suma, Mary Canady and Cindy Thelen for all their input and support.

I am blessed to have the support of my awesome husband Ed. He tolerates me in all the projects I dream up, never complaining I need to get away from the computer and help him a little bit. He has been my best friend for half a century, and I certainly would not be who I am now without having him by my side all these years.

And, of course, I thank my Guides. They seem to have stepped up to the front in the past few years and made themselves known to me. They are instrumental in keeping me positive, calm, joyful, and *sane!* Their guidance has made a profound difference in my life, and I am so grateful.

CONTENTS

PREFACE

I have been writing in journals for years, mostly just documenting our activities—more like a diary. But as the years went by, I shifted into writing to process upsetting events in my life. I even got to the point that when I would start a new journal, I put a note at the beginning to say my life was not always a mess, I just mostly wrote when I needed to work out my feelings.

In 2001, I documented some interesting revelations I attributed to my inner guidance. By 2002, I started to recognize I have a group of guides communicating with me. They are like a council of advisors, a "board of directors." I don't have any names for any of them—they asked me if the main reason I needed a name was so my ego would be able to brag about who was talking to me! I laughed—knowing that was probably true!

These messages come in the form of thoughts in my mind that very easily could be attributed to *me,* not any kind of message from a higher level. However, as I would write out the messages, I noticed I would switch from the pronoun "I" to "we." For example: "What do I need to know about this?" (My own thoughts) "You are doing a great job releasing your resentments and fears. We have chosen you for this assignment, and we are proud of your efforts." (Message from my Guides) It would not be a message from my own thoughts using "we" and "you."

Here is an example of a message I received after I asked what I am supposed to be doing (this came in before I got a message about creating the Arizona Enlightenment Center):

Be aware that you ARE getting yourself ready. You are clearing, clearing, clearing, and doing a great job of it! You will be able to use it all very soon. Just keep exposing your-

self to ideas that raise your consciousness. Every day you are moving up. Even when you take a step backward, you learn and allow yourself to move forward again in a new direction. You are so teachable! Patience is another virtue you are learning. Relax! You will have exactly enough time to do what you are supposed to do in this lifetime. Everything is perfect—exactly how it is supposed to be! Relax! Enjoy! You are doing well to just gather life experiences. You will soon know exactly what to do.

I am sharing in this book many of the messages from my Guides that can be enlightening to you as well. They will appear with an asterisk and in italics so you will know they are a personal message. They are universal truths I have received as I sit quietly, ask questions and record the answers in my journal. I am also including wisdom I have gleaned from numerous workshops and books. Enjoy!

Heather M. Clarke

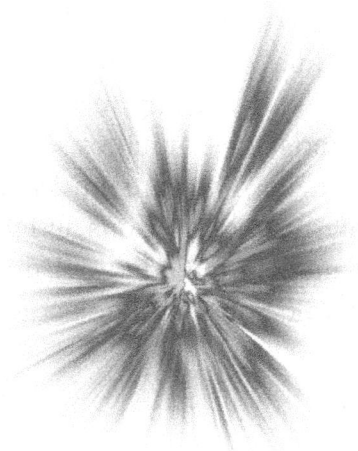

INTRODUCTION

P eople are in a hurry today. They can't conceive of taking the time to check something out—to read a full book—to unclutter their house. Everyone is operating at 100 mph.

I have to confess I am one of these people. If an email will take more than 30 seconds for my reply, it gets put on the back burner, and then a couple of days later, I realize I formulated a response in my mind but totally forgot to type it out and hit Send.

I have been saving up titles for the chapters of my book for *months*, so when the time came, all I had to do was read the title and write the chapter. The problem was, though, I got totally bogged down with the idea I had to write out a bunch of pages on each topic—so of course, I just put it down and went off to do something else.

I finally set an appointment with myself to drive up to the mountains in northern Arizona so I could sit still, get quiet, and let the inspiration flow through me. I was guided to write a book of my stories—make them each no more than two pages—and each with a "bottom line"—a moral to the story. You can read the entire book in less than two hours, or you can put it in the bathroom and read few pages every time you stop by. I was tempted to include a lot more stories (probably just to make the book look bigger!), but I decided to keep it at 44 because once again, I *know* you are busy. These stories have all moved me along my path to "waking up." Open to any story and hopefully you will receive some tidbits of inspiration that will help *you* on *your* path.

You might want to order the *You ALREADY Know This—Guidebook* (www.OriginalInspirationPublishing.com) when you are ready to remember how to re-connect with your inner guidance. It's time!

YOU CAN HAVE ANY OUTCOME YOU CHOOSE

"Yes, you can have _____ (whatever you want), just as soon as you are ready to handle it."

- Rev. Edwene Gaines

One of the most life-altering realizations you can have is you are so powerful you can have whatever you want. *You* have created the life you are living right now—along with all the suffering, sadness, pain, loss, limitations, joy, love, fulfillment, and exhilaration that can go with it. I know, I know, you certainly would not have *chosen* to live with a true jerk or to have a hateful boss, or have your kids reject you. But, guess what? You did! So if you can create that, why not *choose* a happy dream over a nightmare?

There is a scene in the movie *What the Bleep Do We Know* where the leading lady walks down the sidewalk in a lovely park and comes across a teenager bouncing basketballs—hundreds of basketballs—all at the same time. She stops to look at him and when he sees her, he throws her a ball. When she catches it, all the other balls disappear. I interpret this to mean every possible outcome in any situation exists "out there," and the one that comes into your life is the one you focus on and catch when it comes your way. You can catch the ball of the house burning down, of someone stealing all your valuables, of your identity being stolen, or you can catch the ball of owning a thriving business, of having a loving mate, of being financially independent, or of being able to help a lot of people through your personal efforts that bring you total joy. It is all your choice.

Recently, as I was waiting to receive the funds from a huge donation coming in to the Arizona Enlightenment Center, I recognized I was a *really* good "wait-er." I had caught the "waiting" ball. I then decided to go back to the "park" and put the "waiting" ball down and catch the "funding" ball! It was time to move forward with our project, and we didn't need to wait anymore.

Some people get all nervous about having a lot of money come into their life. They are sure they will be the victim of kidnappers or wealth managers who take advantage of them so they will end up losing all the money. Once again—your choice. You are *powerful.* You have no clue how powerful you are. There is no accident you are on the planet at this very transformational time in the history of humanity. You are here for a reason. All you need to do is be willing to step up so you can make your own unique contribution.

~~∽∾⊙⃔∘∣∘⊙⃕∽∾~~

BOTTOM LINE: What do you *want* to happen?
Focus on that and do not allow anything that does not look like what you want to take up any space in your mind or in your vision.

WE ARE ALL UNDER CONSTRUCTION

We are like a block of clay being shaped every day into an exquisite sculpture. We are under construction and the job isn't finished yet.

The roads in Phoenix are constantly being repaired. I have always thought the "Road Construction Union" has a contract with Maricopa County that some part of Indian School Road is required to be under construction at all times. Recently I drove home from a conference and had to get off I-10 because of construction, so I went north to Indian School Road. Then I had to get off Indian School because of construction, so I went south to Osborn Road. Then we crept through that neighborhood with everyone else who was on the detour. Then I got on Camelback Road and had to get off again because it was also under construction!

I live just a house away from a small lake in my neighborhood that recently had to be drained in order to replace some of the retaining wall. It was fascinating to watch the process—especially when you watch people who know how to do the job and have the right equipment. They had to drain the water (which took almost a month!), remove the fish and turtles, scrape away the 8-10 inches of sludge and haul it away, replace some of the dirt, rebuild the wall, install new water aerators, install new lighting, build a new dock, lay down a new sidewalk, refill the lake, restock it with fish, etc., etc. It took almost a year to get it all done, but every step had to be taken in order so the finished product would be perfect. Everyone had to have infinite patience, knowing it really was going to get done.

Our lives are just like this—we are a project. We have to have things drained out of us and sludge removed and walls rebuilt and new systems installed, so we will be perfect when we are done. That is why we are here on the planet. We have come to be reconstructed into the infinite beings we really are, but we have forgotten that is who we are. And we are very carefully guided to the people "who know how to do the job and have the right equipment." We are being re-wired to be able to handle everything coming our way in the future.

∞

BOTTOM LINE: Keep your eyes open so you
will recognize your teachers when they show up.
You have asked for them, and they will appear when
you are ready for the change.

HOLDING THE VISION OF THE ARIZONA ENLIGHTENMENT CENTER

*Sometimes, the bigger the purpose,
the bigger the fear. It is exciting not to know
what you are supposed to do!*

My husband Ed and I had been Realtors for over 20 years when we realized we had enough money saved up that we didn't *have* to work anymore. I remember that day—we both just stood in the middle of our office, feeling like the rug had been pulled out from under us. If we weren't Realtors anymore, *who* would we be? We felt lost, yet we felt excited about what was coming.

Back in 2004, I got a message from Cathy Stuart, an intuitive friend of mine, saying there was going to be a center out here on the west side of the Phoenix area, and she could see me being the hostess, opening the doors and welcoming everyone. It is supposed to be *huge*, and we will have more trouble making it big enough than coming up with the money. The money will just come to us in a miraculous way.

Since I didn't have to "work" anymore, I was totally fired up to get on with it. I had nothing to hold me back: our dogs had died, our kids were grown and fully self-sufficient, I had a very supportive husband. I was so ready to manifest this place. However, for years, the messages I kept getting were telling me it was not yet time. The people who were going to help me were not even here yet. The energies were not fully aligned. I got really tired of hearing I need to WAIT. I wanted so bad to get the center open. I was supposed to keep meeting people and experiencing different healing modalities while things were being pulled together.

For twelve years, basically all I talked about was the Center. I was identified with it with everyone who knew me. I felt like I was "keeping the campfire burning," and I refused to ever lose faith it would eventually be here. I just *know* it is coming. Actually it is already here, we just haven't tuned into it yet. It has been an amazing test of my faith, and I never wandered away from the vision. I always said when the Center does open up, I will write a book about the process. Before it could appear, I knew I had to clear any limitations I had that might block it. I was afraid of it for a long time because it is going to be so big, but I was assured I will not be running it alone. I knew eventually the wisdom I will need to handle this would awaken in me, and I will know what to do.

You are wise to want to sit in the quiet. That is where you will hear us. You have seen how fast things are manifesting for you, so know this is happening in divine timing. Just keep tweaking the vision. That will help it to come into manifestation. It's OK to start small in a rental property and then grow into the larger place. But don't limit your dream. You wouldn't be dreaming it if we had not planted the seeds in your mind—and the others' minds. It has begun. It is on the way. You'll be ready when the time is right!

***

BOTTOM LINE: Success is easy—
just bite off more than you can chew and go do it!

WE ARE HAVING
A LITTLE PARKINSON'S
ADVENTURE

*You never know what you need to know
until you are right in the middle of
needing to know it.*

In 2008, Ed was really not doing well. It was like he was "failing to thrive." He was very weak and frail, and I was not sure what to do about it. I didn't know whether to take him to a naturopathic doctor or an "RD" (a Regular Doctor). I finally decided to take him to our RD just to see what was going on.

As we described his symptoms, the doctor referred us to a neurologist so we could "rule out" Parkinson's Disease. Well, of course, he ruled it *in.* Ed's first comment to me was he was sorry I was going to have to deal with it. His second comment was that since there was no test to prove he had it, he did not have to buy into it. Since it was very mild at the beginning, we were able to go through about three years in denial. We refused to "own" it. I never said my husband had Parkinson's; I would say he had been diagnosed with Parkinson's.

I never expected I would end up being a caregiver. I don't remember signing up for it when I was planning my soul experiences before I came into this life. I think I was in line to get the assignments and was not paying attention because I was talking to someone else in line, so I had no idea what I was raising my hand for. We have been blessed to have awesome caregivers just "show up" for us. Pat, Trish and Felicia are all angels. I couldn't do this without them.

I have had to make major shifts in my life because I do run at 100 mph and he is going at about 5. I often have to slow down or back up so he can catch up with me. It is teaching me to be endlessly patient. Any time I get frustrated and annoyed (at the situation, not at him), I remind myself he would take care of me with infinite patience and love.

Watching the progression of this disease is interesting. It is hard for me to get past the fact he used to be a fighter pilot and now he can hardly make a phone call. But we as a family are so blessed he is not depressed. He does not sit here and say "poor me." We were filling out a Parkinson's Alliance survey about swallowing difficulties and one question was asking how he rates his quality of life. I immediately wanted to mark "fair," but his response was "good"! What a teacher he is!

In 2001 when we went to Doreen Virtue's Hawaiian Healing Retreat, she gave a 15-minute reading to every participant. It is the first and only reading Ed ever had. One of the things he remembered she told him was, "Many years down the road, Heather will be taking care of you." Ha! Here we are—16 years later.

BOTTOM LINE: It is interesting how your life plans can change when you are not looking.

YOU ARE A MASTER MANIFESTOR

Nothing can stop an idea whose time has come.

Years ago, Ed really wanted a red Mazda RX7. We were into goal setting and positive thinking, so one day he cut out a picture of one and taped it to the fridge. An RX7 was not exactly in our plans any time soon, since we could not add another monthly payment to our life at that time. A few weeks later, we went to a car show and realized we really *could* have one if we leased it. So we headed over to the dealership to pick one out. He saw a red one and then a silver one. He went back to the red one and then got pulled back to the silver one. Back and forth—he finally settled on the silver one, and we proudly drove it home. He was surprised he chose the silver one since he *always* loved red sports cars. Then he looked at the picture taped to the fridge—exactly the model and *color* of the one we leased!

Another time, I was getting ready to head out on a Saturday morning to find a piece of plastic that would match the covering over the light bulbs in the dome ceiling in our kitchen. I was intending Home Depot or Lowe's would have just what I needed. Before I was ready to go, the doorbell rang and standing there was a guy from *ARIZONA DOME CEILINGS*, coming to install a unit for our neighbors on the street just behind us! I asked him to come on in and he proceeded to change out all the coverings so the color would match, and then he went to our neighbor's house! It cost $400, but hey! Who would have ever thought that could happen!!?

When you think of something you really want, just ask for it—but remember to ask specifically. When you are on a cruise and you order lunch through room service, you call up and say, "I would like a cheeseburger, medium rare, on a wheat bun with catsup and mustard, tomato and lettuce and pepper jack cheese. I would also like some fries and ketchup, a couple of pickle spears and a glass of ice tea with lots of ice."

Then you hang up, *knowing* your order will be filled. You don't go into the kitchen and follow the cook around to be sure it gets done right. You just wait patiently for the Universe to align the energies of your request and deliver it to your particular room. Everything in life is like that. Put in your specific order and stand back and wait for it to materialize.

<hr />

BOTTOM LINE: What do you really want?
Set your intention and allow it to show up.

WHAT DO YOU CALL GOD?
*If you can't relate to the name "God,"
pick some other name. Choose what makes
you feel comfortable.*

All religions have an aspect of truth. The Dalai Lama once said all light bulbs are valuable. Sometimes a 25-watt bulb is the best and sometimes a 100-watt bulb is appropriate. The reason there are so many different religions in the world is because every time there was a disagreement in the interpretation of the "truth," a group would break away so they could start a new sect. (A new "sect-ion" of the belief system.) This is similar to the different languages all over the world. Everyone has different words to describe the same thing. Almost all religions have forgiveness, love and compassion at the base of their teachings. We are all saying close to the same thing but using different words, even if we do not follow an organized religion.

There are an amazing number of names for "God." Some of them may elicit a reaction in you due to an experience you had in the past, so choose one that does not trigger you. I have an issue with the name "Jesus," but I am very comfortable with the name "Jeshua." So that is what I use. Some people can't handle the word "God." If that name gets the hair on the back of your neck to stand up, pick another name. You can call it Samantha if you want. God doesn't care. I have come up with "GUDSSATI," which to me is a collection of names: **G**od, **U**niverse, **D**ivine, **S**pirit, **S**ource, **A**ll-That-**I**s. There is no baggage attached to that name.

There are an infinite number of paths to "God" or Home or Love. You can get to Flagstaff by going north on I-17, or you can go through Wickenburg and Prescott. It doesn't matter at all to GUDSSATI how you get there. Pick a path that is comfortable to you and go on home.

Back when I first discovered New Thought, *A Course in Miracles,* metaphysics, I was worried maybe I was being misguided and going in a direction that was "wrong." I was attending a traditional church in my neighborhood as well as the Southwest Miracles Center, a center based on *A Course in Miracles* principles. I spoke to the minister, Hal Lafler, asking his advice as to what I should do. He said, "What do you think you will do if you wake up one day and decide you are on the wrong path?" I said I would probably change paths. He said, "Exactly. Go where you feel comfortable and when it is no longer comfortable there, find a different place to go. Each place is exactly where you should be for the moment until it isn't anymore. Each place will contribute to your growth." Many of us are moving away from organized religion into spirituality. But here is another opportunity, just like with politics, to allow everyone to follow whichever path feels right. And especially it is OK not to be called onto any religious or spiritual path. Truth is true and there is no requirement for you to believe it to make it true. It will just continue on being Truth.

BOTTOM LINE: GUDSSATI will wait
patiently for as long as it takes for every one
of us to come on back home.

WHAT AM I SUPPOSED TO BE DOING HERE?

"I have never begun any important venture for which I felt adequately prepared."

- Sheldon Kopp

~~~≈≈≈○≀⊙○≈≈≈~~~

(A message from my Guides):

*You have said it yourself: you are petrified of your real power and purpose. You are waking up slowly and every time these emotionally-charged issues boil up, it is an opportunity for you to heal. That is why they are coming up—it is time to let go of them.

This is your dream. Why would you choose conflict? You know inside what is happening. You just haven't been able to take the steps that will lead you to peace. You owe it to your world to think loving thoughts. You are allowing your ego to run rampant.

How do you move into your power? Just do it. Try things and be surprised at how well they go.

You wonder why you won't take the steps that will move you into your purpose. You think it is because you are afraid. You need to get over this fear quickly so you can do your divine assignment in the world. Stop delaying. Fear is your excuse for not getting on with it. Go ahead and let go of the side of the pool. You will be protected as you get into the flow of your life.

When you focus on why you are doing it, you will understand you are doing it because you are willing to go out and share the knowledge from your life experiences you

14

have gathered over the years so you can affect lives. Your words (which your Guides will give you) will be able to help people receive the divine insight they need to be able to move into their true purpose. This is not about you. It is about how your words will help others to open to their own power so they can also step up and spread the word to those they touch. This is "Pay It Forward."

You think if you do step up and maybe start speaking or giving workshops you might get a "big head" and think you are doing it for the ego satisfaction, that you are pretty cool. Well, if you do allow yourself to step up and own your true purpose, you will make people feel better, so of course you will think you are pretty cool—because you are!

BOTTOM LINE: *What's the alternative?* Not *working in your full purpose? Speaking and thinking you aren't do-ing anything for anybody? Saying* NO *to the Universe?*

YOU ARE THE STORIES YOU TELL

"When telling your story becomes boring to YOU, you know you are ready to move on."

- Dr. Joseph Dillard

I'll bet you have friends (acquaintances) who are well known for their constant gloom-and-doom trauma/drama stories. You get to where you try to avoid eye contact with them so you won't get pulled down into the depths with them—again. You don't want to answer their phone calls, and you ignore them as much as you can.

I know I have been guilty of this myself over the years, and I appreciate the patience of my friends who willingly joined with me as I repeated my latest misery. I eventually quit beating myself up for not being "spiritual" enough to get past it. I finally recognized basically I was just not ready to get over it. I needed a little more time to process it. I would write out my feelings in my journal so I could release the intensity of them and help myself move back into peace.

One day, I was reading through old journals and realized I was writing the *same* stories two years later! I was a broken record. I was also almost addicted to getting advice from friends, teachers, books, movies, etc. I was taking every class that showed up and trying every different healing modality that might help release the drama. Finally, in one week, I was telling the story yet again *three* more times and all three people yawned in my face! One teacher, one fellow student and one friend! I just smiled internally. It was time to tell a different story! Keep telling the same story of drama and you will keep yourself stuck in low vibrations—and you won't be able to attract high vibrational experiences. Realize you tell these stories to get others to agree with your side of the controversy.

Pay attention to the kind of energy coming off the shows you are watching on TV. Sometimes I just have to get out of the room if Ed is watching a violent western or war movie. I can't stand to watch a show where someone is being cruel and inhumane to someone else. I didn't realize it until recently the show is putting out a very low-level vibration. Pay attention to the level of vibration where you hang out. If you aren't happy there, you can change it. Watch only uplifting TV shows or movies, listen to beautiful music, spend time with friends who you *like* to be around, spend time outside in nature. You can raise your vibration by watching only uplifting TV shows or movies, listening to beautiful music, spending time with friends who you *like* to be around, or spending time outside in nature.

***

BOTTOM LINE: Same book, different chapter.
Turn the page! Pick up a different book.

WHAT'S HAPPENING WITH OUR COUNTRY?

Everyone is doing what he thinks is right,
or he would be doing something else.

There has been a lot of conflict and stress in our country lately. The election of 2016 brought out a lot of issues. What I learned in that election campaign is our country is made up of a very diverse group of people. And we seem to be divided about 50/50 to the right or to the left. This is why the country seems to be so divided, no matter *who* is president. This is why our elections are always so close. It would be a rare thing for a candidate to receive a huge majority of the votes. It is almost not even possible. We are so opinionated about everything, and we think if you don't agree with us, you are the one who is wrong.

One solution is we all could allow every other person to have his or her own unique perspective. Everyone thinks his opinion is the right one—or he would change it. *Everyone* thinks he is right. Saddam Hussein thought he was right. Osama bin Laden thought he was right. When you get into a "conversation" with anyone else—most likely about politics—see if you can bite your tongue and let that other person express whatever he needs to express. Don't interrupt or jump in with your version. Don't try to make him wrong. Let him talk. And you can have an agreement he will give you a chance to also express. Get a commitment from the other person that you will each have an opportunity to share safely. See if you can express your opinion without any emotion. Say it just as an observation about what happened. Say it without any outrage or "I-told-you-so" attitude in your voice. Be willing to understand the other side.

Everyone seems to be so separate from each other based on political or religious principles. But I keep thinking about how everyone really could be a helpful neighbor or co-worker if all the opinions and prejudices were removed. If you were hit by a car or if you fell down in a store, people would come to your aid and stay with you until you are stabilized. It doesn't matter then what religion you are or what political party you belong to. We are all basically human, and we are capable of helping someone else who might be in need.

I look at some of the really radical far right or far left people who are active in the political scene and who seem so unreasonable and hateful, and I visualize them being really fun to have over for a backyard barbeque. Let's be vigilant for opportunities to get along with each other. What we really need is a Common Sense Party where every view is given consideration as we work toward a compromise—and all elected officials agree to serve no more than six years—just as our Founding Fathers intended when our country was formed.

❦

BOTTOM LINE: Are you part of the solution
or part of the problem?

IT'S TIME TO CLEAN UP THE DARK SPOTS

The only reason this turmoil is showing up in your life AGAIN is because it is ultimately time to let go of it and clear it out of your life.

I suppose you might have noticed our country was in a great deal of turmoil surrounding the 2016 presidential election. This happens to us every four years. By the time it is over, we feel like we have been assaulted, and you will have a hard time finding anyone who is not in shock about how it was going that year. The part that bothers me the most is to see how much racism, hatred and resentment is still alive and well in the hearts of many of our fellow Americans. It is very disappointing.

However, I have learned to step back and become an observer so I can impartially watch how things turn out. There is great opportunity for healing when these types of events rise up.

Watching all the protests on both sides reminds me of a two-year-old child throwing a temper tantrum, trying to get something after Mom said no. It is a wise mother who can completely remove herself from the drama (become an observer) and let the child work through the frustrations.

If you have some dark stains on your carpet in your living room and you keep your draperies closed, you won't even realize they are there. But when you open the draperies and let the light shine in, the darkness becomes very visible. Only then will you be able to clean up the stains. The darkness (racism?) could have been hanging out there for years without anyone noticing it. But as the dark stains in the world get exposed, the growing Light that is increasing on the planet is able to clean it all up.

All the chaos, terrorism, injustice, and sadness is coming up basically because we are *willing* to go deeper to heal our lives. So in fact, it is good this is being stirred up now and certain people are doing a great job shaking it all up so we can finally be rid of it.

⚜

BOTTOM LINE: You can't remove the darkness
if you don't know it is there.

STOP REHEARSING A GATHERING STORM

"If you knew who walks beside you on this path that YOU have chosen, you would never feel fear again."

- A Course in Miracles

❧

Many of your "problems" stem from your inability to say what is on your mind. When you step into your power, you will have no fear about talking to anyone and saying what is inside—and you can deliver it all with love. Set your intention for how you will show up in the world, and *nothing* will be able to threaten or harm you.

If you were 100% positive you would be successful, what would you do now that is different from what you have always been doing? Be willing to be guided in a different direction, even if you are freaking out about going that way. Dannion Brinkley has said, "Make *fun* of everything that scares you."

I can remember a girl in my 6th grade class named Pam who had full-grown adult-sized confidence. I can remember just watching her and wishing I could be like her. At that age and on through high school, I was afraid to express my own opinion on anything and always wanted to know what *your* opinion was first so I could say things I knew would have your agreement. I had braces and glasses for four years in junior and senior high school and was just not willing to step out into the limelight and get noticed.

I actually changed when I was a sophomore in college and I got my first pair of contacts. My vision is so bad my glasses are as thick as coke-bottle bottoms. When I put those contacts on, getting rid of the glasses I had since the third grade, I really made a big step up in my confidence. As I got older and more mature, I got to a stage where I could express an opinion without concern whether anyone else agrees with me. I am able to allow the other person to have a different opinion without my getting offended. I don't remember when I shifted out of being afraid to speak in front of a group.

You are a very good person, loving and compassionate. You just have some fear growing inside that makes you make up scenarios that are going to happen in the future. Stop rehearsing gathering storms. The mind loves a chew toy! Give it one that brings you peace. Your ego is very busy. Keep reassuring it that all is well. Send it outside to play so you can hear your guidance.

<hr>

BOTTOM LINE: Nothing frightens fear more than a human without any.

23

CHOOSE ONCE AGAIN

*Look at your life. You are VERY powerful. By the
choices you make, you have created every bit of
your life—the good AND the bad.*

We choose to be angry, depressed or afraid. We can just
as easily decide to be trusting, happy or confident. Any time
you are upset, you are listening to the voice of your ego.
Ask your Guides for a different way to look at the situation
so you can move back into peace. When you help yourself
by being happy, you are helping everyone else. People like
to be around happy, peaceful people. The happier you are,
the more you spread the Light in the world. Choose to bring
the Light into every situation where you find yourself so
everyone around you will be affected by it.

A Course In Miracles teaches this whole world is an illu-
sion—just a dream—and we can change our waking dream
just as easily as we can change our sleeping dream. You
don't have to have upset kids, depressed friends or any kind
of turmoil in *your* dream. You can change it at any moment
by choosing a different outcome.

The very first job I had was with Kelly Girls, a temporary
help agency. I had an assignment for a few weeks typing up
reports for an insurance company. I was a recent college
graduate and had never had a real job, so I was pretty nervous and took a lot of time figuring out what I was supposed
to do. One day, one of the partners walked by my desk and
said, "You really are slow." Now, even back then, I knew I
had a choice—to buy into that comment which would nega-

tively affect me for the rest of my life—or I could choose to completely ignore it. I said to myself he does not know who I am. I was a straight-A student, an excellent typist, very intelligent and a great organizer. Luckily, I chose to stay strong and remind myself he knew nothing about me, so I refused to let him affect my self-image.

There is another well-told story about two brothers who had a father who was a raging alcoholic. The father's drinking kept him from having any success at anything he tried. Many years after the father died, one brother had become extremely successful and the other brother was a hopeless alcoholic. When they were asked why they thought they were where they were in life, the successful brother said, "Well, what do you expect? Look at my father." And the alcoholic brother said, "What do you expect? Look at my father." Choices.

❦

BOTTOM LINE: Be too happy to permit
the presence of trouble.

"HO'OPONOPONO" WHAT IN THE WORLD IS THAT?

I'm Sorry.
Please Forgive Me.
Thank You.
I Love You.

This is a really loose, *Heather-ized* version of what Ho'oponopono is all about. There was a doctor in Hawaii who believed everyone who comes into your life is a product of your own thoughts. So if you interact with someone who is an addict, he believed you are the one who actually created the circumstances of the addiction. When he used Ho'oponopono with a hospital ward full of criminally insane patients, *everyone* was cured and released, yet he never met with a single one of the patients. He worked on healing himself, and it positively affected the patients in the hospital.

His healing modality, Ho'oponopono, has four steps to help heal every person who comes into your field:

1st, I'm sorry. (You have a particular soul lesson to learn in this life and you "bring" someone in to help you. You say, "I'm sorry I need to learn this lesson.")

2nd, Please forgive me. (You say to that person, "Please forgive me for bringing you into my life so I can learn this lesson.)

3rd, Thank you. (Thank you for being willing to help me learn this lesson.)

4th, I love you. (I love you for helping me learn this lesson.)

Take some time to look at who you have attracted into your life. What is the lesson you need to learn? Can you appreciate those people who have shown up for you so you can have the opportunity to grow?

BOTTOM LINE: Learn the lesson quickly so these people can be released from the need to play that role.

BE WILLING TO LET GO OF SOMETHING YOU LOVE

Everyone is playing an essential part
in this intricately-woven Universe.
Just show up and report for duty.
Follow the direction of your Guides.

Way back in 1986, I found the most beautiful, ice-clear quartz crystal as the very first stone in my collection. It fit in my hand perfectly, and I carried it with me most of the time. Since then, when I go into a crystal store, I end up buying yet *another* one that "speaks" to me and compels me to take it home with me.

In 2001, Ed and I went to a healing retreat in Hawaii put on by Doreen Virtue. The first day, we were led through an exercise out on the lush lawn where we were supposed to walk up to something in the area and ask, "Are you my teacher?" When we approached something that seemed to indicate it WAS our teacher, we were to ask if it had a message for us.

When we gathered back under the tent, we were invited to share our stories. One woman in front of me got up and told about this amazing crystalline woman moving through a crystal room, and all of a sudden I heard in my head, "Give her your crystal." My response: "Heck no!" It came again: "Give her your crystal." "NO!" The third time it came, I finally knew I was going to have to give it to her. After the meeting, she got up to go back to her room to get ready to have a swim with the dolphins. I was relieved because that would give me more time to process the whole thing. I stood up to go pick up some tourism information about the island, and there she was, right in front of me! I handed her the crystal saying, "I am supposed to give this to you." She thanked me and went back to her room. I was so upset I couldn't even talk to Ed about it until after dinner that night. During the rest of the week, I never saw her again.

Six months later, I attended Doreen's Angel Therapy Practitioner training in Long Beach. In the middle of the week, several healers and practitioners were allowed to give the class participants some mini-sessions. Carolyn, the woman who now had my crystal, was one of the healers, and I signed up to have a session with her. I ended up being part of a group of seven people receiving the healing together. During the session, I could feel some very powerful pressure on my face. I don't usually feel anything like that. When it was over, I went up to her and told her I was the one who gave her that crystal in Hawaii. Then she said, "Oh my gosh! It is the most powerful crystal I have! Didn't you just feel it in the group?" Then I realized I *had* to get the crystal in her hands so she could use it to heal people—something I would not be doing any time soon.

⁓⦿⦿⦿⁓

BOTTOM LINE: Sometimes we need to be willing to let go of something really important to us because there is a better use for it in someone else's hands.

I DIDN'T KNOW WHAT TO DO

You are amazing…
So what if you make a mistake?

My mother died unexpectedly in 1990 from a brain hemorrhage. I wrote her obituary very quickly to get it into the local paper in time to be published in the next issue to announce the details of her memorial service. She had been a homemaker—a very good homemaker—a choir director, a piano teacher, a Girl Scout leader, a mother of three, a Republican voter registrar—but she never spent years dedicated to a professional career. I didn't know which details to include—and I didn't run it by anyone else in the family before I took it to the newspaper office.

Well, Grandma Falls was *very* upset about how awful the write-up was and mentioned it several times over the years. Finally, I told her I had written it, and since I had never had a mother die before, I didn't know what to do. That pretty much ended that complaint.

What I finally understood was that in this situation, I made the choice to not feel guilty for life for that obituary because I really had never been in that situation before, so why would I expect to know what to do? There is nothing I can do to change any of it, so it does not serve me to continue to carry guilt about it. If I were in that situation again today, would I know what to do now? Of course I would. I learned from those mistakes so I can do a better job the next time.

A baby does not know how to do algebra. He needs to grow up first and have some experiences that will help him get ready for that new concept. We don't condemn the baby because he doesn't know what to do with an algebra problem.

<hr>

BOTTOM LINE: If you knew what to do, you would have done it. You are always doing the best you can.

ARE YOU A VIBRATIONAL MATCH?

*Who and what are you choosing
to spend your life energy on?
Is it a good match?*

~~~❦~~~

Everything has its own vibration. *Everyone* has a unique vibration. Some vibrations don't blend together harmoniously.

This is one reason people get a divorce. Through the years, each person grows and expands in unique ways, and eventually the changes can cause conflicts in the relationship. Years ago, I knew of a woman who had been married four times. At first, I was pretty judgmental about it, but then I realized each divorce had been caused by the fact she and her husband had changed and were no longer a vibrational match. It was just time to move on.

Any time I come across a person I don't relate to or who I might want to avoid, I now understand we are just not a vibrational match. I may be vibrating at a C and she may be vibrating at a D Flat. The C and the D Flat separately are perfectly fine sounds, but together, they don't make a harmonious chord. The C is not wrong and the D Flat is not wrong. They just don't work well together, so it is time to move on to a different note.

I am sure you have heard people describe someone as a "real low life." They don't realize they are recognizing the lower vibration in that guy. You can feel the energy of other people without even knowing it. Pay attention now that you have read this and see how your inner guidance helps you be discerning about who you are hanging out with.

Family members give us plenty of opportunity to grow. They can either be a source of great love and support or they can be a source of stress and pain. Actually, your biological family is NOT necessarily your spiritual family—and it is OK to pull away and spend more time with people who do make you feel nurtured and supported. We are conditioned in our culture that we are supposed to be loyal and connected to our family, but in fact, if they cause you excessive distress and anxiety, you owe it to your own peace of mind to withdraw and plug your energy into a new group where you can continue your growth.

However, it is important to your growth that you are able to pull away from those who no longer serve you with love rather than with resentment. If you leave and continue to think of them with resentment, you really have not let go of them.

BOTTOM LINE: The greatest gift you can offer the world is your peace of mind, and you will have greater peace of mind when you are around people who are a vibrational match to you.

I AM SUCH A GOODY-GOODY

If you do something now that is out of integrity, you ARE going to get exposed.

~~~

I have been a goody-goody my whole life. I am a rule follower. I tell the truth. If a door says "Do Not Enter," I do not enter! If I make an insurance claim for something I lost and later find it, I return the claim money. In 1956, we got the Encyclopedia Americana for Christmas, and I was ecstatic! I loved to do reports in school and that was like having the internet of the 1950s in our own home.

When I was six or seven, my brother Johnie and a couple friends decided it would be cool to make little match guns out of clothespins and shoot burning matches through the rafters in our garage into the storage room. Little Miss Goody-Goody had to have the hose ready and available just in case something happened. And of course, something happened! Mom really freaked out about that!

When I was 11, our whole gang of friends would go out to our fort in the woods and smoke and then eat peppermint candies on our way home so we wouldn't smell like cigarettes. Later we did it at home when our parents were out, and we even had our little sister Debbie do it too so she wouldn't tell on us. The only problem was we left all the cigarette butts and ashes in all the ashtrays on the patio. No way to deny that and get away with it. So we got shut down on that little experiment. It was the Universe redirecting me so I would *not* become a smoker. As much as I tried, I just couldn't inhale.

I have to admit one time I actually *did* lie to my dad. I was a teenager and one night a couple kids in the neighborhood came over when my parents were gone. We helped ourselves to a few drinks of the bourbon Dad always had in a decanter on the counter. The next day, Dad asked me if we had gotten into it (since some of it was obviously missing!). I remember immediately cycling through all possible outcomes if I told the truth, and I flat-out lied. I still can't believe it. And I never did fess up to them before they died. Luckily, the calm, wise voice in my head reassured me it was OK to lie just that one time since I was such a goody-goody!

For the past several years we have been in a place in the progression of humanity that can be called the "Age of Integrity." It is part of the Mayan Calendar. Just watch the news and see how so many celebrities, government officials and top businesspeople have been arrested. It is a lot harder now to get away with anything because *everyone* has a cell phone with a camera. It has resulted in a major shift in the integrity of the world. GUDSSATI has set that up.

BOTTOM LINE: If you decide to tell a lie, you have to have a really good memory so you can remember what you said to which person.

35

YOU ARE SAFE WHEREVER YOU ARE

When you help yourself by being happy, you are helping everyone else. People like to be around happy, peaceful people. The happier you are, the more you spread the light in the world.

~~~

People spend a lot of time worrying about the future and how what is going on in the world can adversely affect every aspect of their lives.

I have always felt if you did not know what was going on, you could just continue with your own life and be as happy and carefree as you always have been. We were on a long 10-week camping trip in 2005, and we got home two days before Hurricane Katrina hit Louisiana. Now, if we were still driving all over our magnificent country, not watching TV or listening to the news on the radio, we would have no clue anything happened. It was the same thing with the 9/11 attacks.

I have a plan in case a major natural disaster or some kind of terrorist attack happens in downtown Phoenix: we will pack up several picnic meals, some sleeping bags, our "grab-n-go" survival pack I have in each of our cars, a couple chairs and little camping tables and head up to White Tank Park, just 20 minutes northwest of our house. We can sit out there in the stunning glory of our Arizona desert and play cards, read a book, listen to some music, and *know* we are completely safe.

You are not always affected by every negative event

that happens in the world. You can be sitting in your house which is full of love and high vibrational energy while four houses down the street, the couple is fighting—again—he hits her and she falls down. The kids are screaming, the dog is upset, and you have no idea that is even going on. You are living in a frequency where you can't comprehend what is happening where the other family is living. It is not a "lower" frequency, a "bad" frequency, just a different frequency, and each person in this story has chosen the vibrational level to live in at that particular moment.

None of this implies you are insensitive and have a lack of compassion. I am just pointing out you don't have to be affected by every negative event that happens in the world because you can vibrate at a different level and be in a place where you cannot connect with the negative frequency of the event. Focus on keeping yourself at a very high level, and you will attract other high-level vibrational experiences into your life.

BOTTOM LINE: Either GUDSSATI is going to take care of you or not—your choice.

ALLOW NO DOUBT

It is time to leave all doubts behind.

The Arizona Enlightenment Center has taken 12 years to manifest—so far. As I write this in early 2017, it is still not here, yet I *know* it is coming. I am very experienced in holding down the fort. I know how to do it, and I *know* it will eventually manifest.

Throughout the years of holding the vision of the Center, I was reminded over and over to be patient, don't force anything to happen, allow things to align. You can't deliver a baby at seven months and expect it to be fully developed. You have to give it the full nine months. Be patient. Relax. Have faith. *Know* it. We are at eight months, three weeks, and five days.

A couple years ago, I washed one of my contacts down the drain, requiring me to go through the drill of getting new ones. I had heard about a local university where they train eye doctors, dentists, and veterinarians. I decided to give them a try. But after two weeks of waiting, the new contacts turned out to not be a good prescription. I needed to go back, so I decided to go to my regular eye doctor to get his prescription to see how it compared to the one from the school. This took another 10 days to get an appointment. I thought this could be a good teaching moment for the student doctor if his prescription was significantly off from my doctor's reading. It turned out to be slightly off, and I was able to order a new pair through the school. More weeks went by as I waited for them. I got the replacement—still wrong! Another delay. I finally ordered some from my regular doctor and *more* weeks went by.

It ended up taking three months to get a good pair, yet during all the delays, I was completely confident that eventually I would get my new contacts. I never allowed any kind of doubt to sneak in, because I *knew* they were coming. The energy just needed to be aligned for the right prescription.

BOTTOM LINE: As I wait patiently for the manifestation of the Arizona Enlightenment Center, I do not entertain any doubt. I do not set a place for it at my table. I *know* it will manifest, as soon as the energy is aligned. I refuse to allow the energy trying to "pull me off the bus" to take control of me. I keep my focus on what I *want* to happen.

WAIT! LET ME DO THIS FIRST

"Your ego's delay tactics include addictive behaviors such as television viewing, internet surfing, reading newspapers...to drown out God's voice when you are not ready to receive it. Deep down you realize they are monumental wastes of time."

- Doreen Virtue

I am really good at keeping myself occupied with lots of unnecessary busy-ness. I take on all kinds of projects, spending hours analyzing things, planning events, devoting time to organizing the piles of papers in my house.

Being a Virgo means I am very interested in details, so I enjoy paying the bills and keeping track of all the expenses. I loved the first of the month when I could go through the pile of bills and receipts and record them all in my Quicken account. I even recognized that having to pay all those bills kept me working as a Realtor. Why keep working so hard if we don't have a lot of bills to pay? Ed finally said, "Why don't you shift your focus to handling our investments instead of our debts?" (He is so wise!) I did that, and it completely shifted our financial situation.

Sometimes, it is almost a relief when one of my teams loses—the Suns or the Cardinals. I got to the point where I would record a game, find out if they won, and if not, I could save all those hours spent watching the whole thing. *And* I could save all the time I usually spent reading the sports page because I didn't want to hear about what was wrong with the team. When they would win, I would watch the local newscast on Channel 3, 5, 10, 12 and 15 just to bask in the glory of the story. Ed would walk by and ask me if they still won as I watched all the different stations. So if they lost, I could save all that time too. Sports, in general, play the role of keeping us distracted from what would probably be more important to invest our time and energy in—writing a book, for example.

I have noticed I have been getting message after message for the past few years telling me it is essential for me to take some time every day—even if it is just 10 minutes—to sit down, clear my mind, just be quiet and get away from the TV, the phone and the computer. One of these days, I will *get* it—that this is the most important thing I can do. I realize I have my priorities all wrong. If I want to connect more with my Guides to get my answers and inspiration, I need to make that my highest priority. But I see I do all the little things on my to-do list first. Maybe I think I need to get everything done first and *then* I can go sit down—and of course, I never get the to-do list done, so I usually don't get to the meditation time.

∽⌒◯⟨ᆺ⟩◯⌒∾

BOTTOM LINE: Pay attention to what you are focusing on. Is it moving you forward toward your next goal or is it allowing you to delay it one more day? What are you avoiding? That you just might be REALLY powerful? That you have a big part to play in the world right now?

WELL, THAT WAS EASY!

Each one of us has some excuse for not putting our life into action. Your spiritual gifts are needed now.

We have had an RV off and on for probably 25 years. Our last one was a 29-foot Minnie Winnie that was just delightful. We went out to all kinds of great places and in 2005, we took a long 10 week trip all over the country visiting family and friends. By the time we got back, I was Miss Organized, since every time you move to a new location, you have to put *everything* in its place so it does not fall as you drive down the road.

Ed always did the driving, and when we got to a campground, we were part of the RV culture of retired Grandmas and Grandpas—the Grandpa slowly backs into the camping spot as the Grandma stands in the back, directing him to turn a little more to the right or left to get into the middle of the space. Sometimes you observe this ritual playing out with much love and patience and other times, Grandpa is up to here with being in that darn camper and needs Grandma to do a better job of directing him into the spot so he can sit down and have a beer.

I was always afraid to drive the RV since it was so long. I even had a dream about it. I dreamed I ended up actually driving it, and as I got out on to the freeway, I could feel the fear building up in my heart I had bitten off more than I could chew. But it was too late, I couldn't go back. I had to stay far over in the right lane so everyone else could pass me, and I didn't change lanes unless I had to. If you ever saw the movie *Clueless,* you will understand how scared I was when you see Alicia Silverstone's best friend accidentally get onto the freeway in Los Angeles when she was just learning how to drive. We were both completely out of control and at the mercy of the other drivers.

A few years ago, I told Ed I thought I needed to know how to drive the RV just in case something happened to him while we were out camping and I would be required to get us home. We went out to the storage yard where we kept it, and I hopped into the driver's seat. I backed it out, drove out of the lot, pulled into a gas station to fill up, and then *backed into our driveway.* Holy Moses, did I feel powerful! But the real revelation is that it turned out to be so easy. It didn't scare me at all, and I never had fear of it again.

BOTTOM LINE: Your fears can seem to be completely overwhelming and unmanageable, but when you get on the other side of that fear, you can accomplish many things you never thought possible.

DON'T FORGET TO ASK

You can manage the circumstances of your life.
Just ask for what you need.

I have a major issue with proper use of commas, quotation marks, apostrophes—so much I can't even read a book that has not been properly proofread. (Virgos can't help it!) You could call me "The Punctuation Cop." The problem with mistakes is they distract the readers from the point of the sentence as they think about what the author "should have said." It is almost a curse, because most of the time, I can't even remember what I read since I am looking for all the periods that need to be *inside* the quotation mark—unless you are British. (OK, now I *know* you will be scanning this book for missing commas!)

Several years ago, I met Chako Priest, who was channeling a book coming through her from a wide variety of Ascended Masters. She finished her first book and printed up just five copies in manuscript form at Staples. For some reason she gave one copy to me. I was surprised because we had only known each other for a couple months. As I started reading it, I kept coming across incorrect sentence structure, incorrect punctuation, and a few typos. I thought since she was just printing up a few copies at a time, I could point out these mistakes and she could correct them for the next copies. I started an email to her with an ongoing list. But, I just couldn't send it to her because I felt it was rather pretentious of me to correct her book without being asked to do it. So I sat on it for a couple weeks until I was able to word it in a joking way and soften my suggestions. Finally, I hit Send.

At the same time, Chako was working on her second book and was so frustrated with it because Microsoft Word kept underlining suggested changes. She was not aware that many times, Microsoft Word's suggested changes have nothing to do with anything. She had just sat back in exasperation, saying, "I need some help here!" And then my email arrived!

BOTTOM LINE: There are "Circumstantial Beings" with us all the time, arranging our lives every day to help us along our path, providing the help we have just asked for. So don't forget to ask.

YOU DON'T NEED
TO "FIX" ANYONE

You don't have to fix the world.
Just fix yourself.

When I used to worry about a friend or family member years ago, I did a meditation where I would put that person in a big gift box and tie it up with a huge beautiful bow. I then put the box on a dolly and rolled it out to the front yard and looked up to Heaven, saying, "OK GUDSSATI, I am sending him to you. I can't do it anymore." Then I saw this huge hand appear out of the clouds and reach down to pick up the box. As it got closer, the box just got smaller and smaller. GUDSSATI was able to pick up that huge, heavy box with no effort at all. That showed me a problem that looked overwhelming to me is a very tiny problem to GUDSSATI. I just need to be willing to let go of it, to let go of trying to fix that person. GUDSSATI is on duty in that person's house, just as much as He is on duty in my house, and if He needs me to help, He will let me know.

Another solution is to give up any expectations you have about someone. When you have expectations, it is very easy to be disappointed with that person's behavior. Let everyone learn his own life lessons. You don't need to fix anyone. Get out of the way and let him experience what life has in mind for him so he can move up the ladder of consciousness. One of my teachers, Dr. Dina Evans, once said, "Don't expect unconscious people to act in a conscious way. They simply don't have the tools yet to make conscious decisions. It is not intentional. What is there to forgive? We are all on the path."

Everyone is on a different rung of the ladder. No one is on a better rung than anyone else. We are all having our own unique life experiences that are waking up our souls.

I have a magnet on my refrigerator that says: For peace of mind, resign as the General Manager of the Universe.

BOTTOM LINE: There is a line in the *A Course in Miracles* that says: "If you would correct your brother, then you must think that correction by you is possible, and this can only be the arrogance of the ego." Ouch!

WHAT IS DYING?

*It is absolutely guaranteed
you will survive your dying.*

I don't have an issue with dying—no fear—no anguish I won't see my family and friends ever again. In my opinion, when we die, I think we just raise our vibration right out of this third dimension into another dimension where pain and disease cannot exist. We get to let go of our compromised bodies full of aches and pains and illnesses and reclaim our youthful 30-year-old bodies.

Dying is shifting from one form to another—like an ice cube (solid) melting into water (liquid) and evaporating (rising up) into air—all the while it is still H2O. You will go from your solid body to a liquid state and then evaporate into spirit—and it is still *you*. But this *you* will be in the form of Who You Really Are—and who you have really been all along.

Just as you are caught by the doctor when you emerge into this life, you fall into the arms of your loved ones when you emerge into the non-physical form of life.

Right before John Adams died, he wrote in a letter to Thomas Jefferson that the body that housed him was tired, falling apart and ready to be laid aside, but he knew *John Adams* was just fine.

Life here on Earth has been an exciting adventure as we learned all the lessons our soul agreed to experience and then we get to put down the tired old body like a suit of clothes, step out of our limitations and *soar*.

I am talking a good game here, because no one has ever

told me I am going to die soon. Check back later and see if I'm so confident then! Ha! (Actually, I don't plan to die—I fully expect to ascend!)

BOTTOM LINE: Dying is really our next great adventure.

YOUR ANSWERS ARE WITHIN YOU

*"You will never be led astray
by your own personal guidance system."*

- Carol Tuttle

Over the years, I have been getting more and more messages from my Guides that I totally count on as being correct. Actually, they HAVE to be correct, or how can you trust any of it?

I wanted to use a pendulum to get answers way back when I first started on this spiritual journey. Some people may think that is a pretty weird thing to do, but it really responds to energy flowing through your subconscious mind. It is also called "dowsing," and often a form of it is used to find water or underground oil, etc. I don't know how it works, but it just does. You can make a pendulum by tying a washer to one end of a string. About 8-12 inches is fine. You just start with holding it in your right or left hand and let it dangle as still as possible. Then you ask a question that can be answered with a yes or no and wait to see which way it starts to swing. One way will indicate NO and the other way will indicate a YES.

I took a class in it a *long* time ago. I simply could not get it to work. The teacher was amazed at how still I could get it, but it just would not move. I decided the pendulum was not one of the ways I was going to get information. After many years, I eventually did develop the ability to use it quite accurately. Some people use one for almost every decision they make.

One Saturday, I saw that an antique store in downtown Phoenix was having an appraiser at the store and I could take two items in to get a value for just a few dollars. My first thought was it would be too crowded and I will waste my Saturday morning if I go down there. I got out *three* pendulums and asked over and over if I should go and the answers were *all yes.*

I drove in town, and sure enough, just as I suspected, the line was out the door, and I would not have been able to hang around all day waiting for my turn. I left the store and as I walked to my car, I asked my Guides what was up with the incorrect guidance from the pendulums?

The answer: *The guidance was NOT wrong. Your very first thought was it would be crowded and you would waste your morning. But you chose to get your answer from something outside of YOU. It was not wrong to tell you to go, because you received the lesson that you did NOT need to go and you already knew that. You do not need the pendulums.*

BOTTOM LINE: Once you learn to trust yourself, you will see you do not need to seek answers from anywhere outside of yourself.

WHAT THE HECK DO YOU DO IN HEAVEN?

Rest is not idleness... To lie sometimes on the grass under the trees on a summer's day, listening to the murmur of water or watching the clouds float across the sky, is by no means a waste of time.

I have always needed to have a reason to be here. I *hate* to be bored. I need a purpose. I thrive on being really busy and getting everything done. I love details. I am most productive if I am working under a deadline.

I realize while I keep myself busy with all my "important" duties, I keep myself from being quiet and calm and mellowed out. I have gotten all kinds of "messages" telling me how essential it is to sit down, be still and meditate even just a few minutes every day. My Guides remind me that I keep asking what I should do next, yet I am buzzing around everywhere which prevents me from hearing them. I have to sit down, shut up and listen! I need to empty my busy mind so they can fill me up with their inspiration.

I finally got it. I put off meditating and sitting in the stillness because it is scary to let myself empty out. It also brings up my concern about what will you do when you get to Heaven if you finally get to have everything you want and do whatever you want. What do you do when there is nothing to work toward or nothing to plan for? It seems to me you would get bored quite quickly if you can have everything and you can do anything. So I can see I don't really look forward to getting there any time soon.

However, my good friend Chako Priest has written two books where she "interviewed" 20 entities (people) after they passed on. She did ask one of them (at my request) about what one does when one gets to Heaven. His reply was it is very fulfilling because you get to do whatever you want to do. All you have to do is think what you want to do and you are there in the middle of doing it. You can do everything you ever wanted to do. This particular person had been a Navy pilot and when he got to heaven, he was able to fly everywhere he could imagine and even help others learn how to fly. He was completely fulfilled.

I was so glad to hear that since it had been such a concern to me over the years! What a relief!

After you pass over into Heaven, you will continue your soul growth, and you will be able to help others in all the ways you have ever wanted to help. You will still be making a big impact on others because you will take on assignments to help.

BOTTOM LINE: Release your fear that if you let yourself wake up, you will lose your identity.

YOU ALREADY KNOW
WHAT THAT SPEAKER IS
GOING TO SAY

Stop looking out there for your answers. Your answers are within. You must be still in order to wake up. The one requirement is to be still.

~~~❧~~~

I have been "waking up" since the mid 80s. My good friend Judy asked me to attend some spiritual development classes at our community church being taught by another friend, Debby. When Judy and I walked into the room for the first time, I burst into tears—it was like "I found it, but I didn't even know I was looking for anything." That began my spiritual journey. I had no clue what metaphysical meant. I never even talked about God or Jesus or anything like that. I became a "workshop-aholic," attending every class, seminar, conference, or lecture that came along for *years*. I was like a sponge, absorbing as much spiritual knowledge and experience as I could.

In 2010, I attended a weekend workshop at Debby's healing center near Dallas. During that weekend, Debby asked if I was open for a message from her. I said I certainly was—I always love getting messages from intuitive people. She is able to see a person's energy fields to be able to help the person understand how to heal. She told me my energy fields were completely stuck and nothing was moving between them. I was stuck full of *knowledge* because I attend so many classes and workshops and read everything I can get my hands on. She said I needed to stop going to any more classes because I already know what will be taught. She suggested I start taking some exercise classes, and completely change how and what I eat.

I definitely heard what she was telling me, so I came home, started taking yoga, started "thinking about" eating differently, and started passing on opportunities to attend another workshop. This lasted several months—and then, a few workshops showed up I *really* wanted to attend. I signed up, hoping God would be busy and not notice I attended! As the years have passed by, I of course have gone back to attending more classes, although I would attend a lot more if I didn't need to have a caregiver for Ed every time I leave home. So he is playing a role of stopping me from overdoing the learning I am so driven to take in.

I had an Ayurevedic astrology reading one time and found out you are more your rising sign than your sun sign. I have Sagittarius rising and apparently that means I will be fascinated with learning everything I can, and the challenge for me in this lifetime is to be able to focus in on a few topics and stop being so scattered by dipping into every topic that comes up that interests me. I want to say to Ed, "Sorry, I *have* to take that class. It's in my chart. I can't help it!"

***

BOTTOM LINE: If we had any idea of *who* we really are, we would *know* we already know!

HOW I FEEL ABOUT AGING

Your age is just a number.
It has nothing to do with you.
The day you turn 80, you are just one day older
than you were yesterday.

I am 71 years old as I write this and I feel like I am about 45. (That would be a little difficult, though, since ours boys are 46 and 44!!) I am full of energy and interested in *everything*. Even though I do notice I have more bodily aches and pains due to some kind of inflammation, I never let it slow me down or keep me from doing anything.

When I remind myself I am past turning 70, it seems to take me by surprise. I keep saying I am actually "youthing" instead of "aging." People tell me I look so young, as do many of my friends. Several are in their 80s and seem like they are in their 60s. I can remember when I was past 21 and still getting "carded" so I could buy a drink. I would say to myself it may be annoying to look so young when I *am* young, but it's going to be great fun to look so young when I am *not* young. Just wait till I'm 70! Well, here I am—in my 70s!

My grandmother lived till she was 99½. She was a real character and loved for me to take her shopping so she could tell everyone who helped her that she was 96 or 97 and then listen to the expressions of amazement. When she died, she looked like she was 50. We had a neighbor in Virginia who has been very active physically way into her 90s. She loves to go to her clogging dance classes. She is not letting old age slow her down.

We all know people who look so much older than their real age. They have made the choice to allow the wear and tear of their lives drag them down and keep them from getting full enjoyment from their life experiences. I remember taking my grandmother to her doctor appointments and watching all the other elderly people coming and going. It was especially hard to watch a little old lady, almost crippled herself, pushing her husband in a wheelchair.

I feel so fortunate to actually feel good at my age, since I am able to enjoy life so much. I can see that if someone does not feel good, it would be very hard to get motivated to get off the couch or out of bed to go do something fun and interesting. I am also blessed to be healthy so I can help take care of Ed as he lives with Parkinson's Disease. Can you imagine what a mess it would be if *both* of us needed caregivers?

BOTTOM LINE:
Look in your mirror and say this to yourself every morning:
I feel happy. I feel healthy.
I feel terrific. Every day in every way
I am getting better and better.
(Pay attention to how this changes your life.)

KILLING OFF MOM

It is not possible to release a part of you that has been ingrained since birth—or even before birth.

I have always been a vivid dreamer. I could remember many, many details that seemed so odd and usually had nothing to do with anything else in the dream. It was like having four or five different "chapters" in any one dream. I used to write them down in a separate dream journal, but after a while, I quit doing it because it would wear me out. Some of them would be over four pages long. It is fun, though, to go back and read them again to see if any seem to have a message for me now.

Years ago, I had a dream that my son Tim and I decided to kill my mother. We had all the details completely planned, and it seemed to be a fairly simple thing to carry out. Tim was going to do the deed and let me know when it was done. Neither one of us had any hesitation about the fact it is just not exactly what one should do to one's mother!

As the time drew near, I did finally start to have my doubts and freaked out I would not be able to get there in time to stop him before he actually did it. I ran to Mom's house hoping to call it off, but I arrived too late. Mom was lying on the living room floor and Tim was standing nearby, holding the gun.

My heart sank as I ran over to her—and then she just got up. She acted like nothing had happened and went on out to the kitchen as if everything was completely normal. What a relief! Tim and I were in shock it looked like we were not going to have to face any dire consequences for our crazy idea.

I had been going through some experiences where I understood I needed to pull back from trying to handle everything for our kids and grandkids. I was ridiculously involved in their lives, and I knew it was time to withdraw to let them have their own life experiences. That is probably why I had that dream. It had nothing to do with actually killing off my mother.

BOTTOM LINE: You really can never kill off the motherhood (or fatherhood) in you. It is not possible. Once you are a mother, you are always a mother, no matter how much you might think you should give up the job. See if you can learn to be a "non-invasive mother"!

A LIFE-LONG FEAR

What life offers today is what I need—
no matter what I think!

As Bud, my favorite dog, got older, I could feel the anxiety building up in me about maybe having to put him down. It had been a life-long fear. I just could not imagine being able to take a pet in to be euthanized. Our other dog, Zildjian, had a heart attack one Sunday afternoon, right on the kitchen floor as we were fixing dinner. Bud was deaf and blind, so I wondered how long it would take for him to notice Zildjian was not around anymore. It took about two days, and he attached himself to me. Even though he couldn't see, he just *knew* when I got up and moved to another room. He would hop up and follow me everywhere.

When I would sit down to meditate, I would be sure to shut the bedroom door tightly because he would come in, pant, lick his paws and be a real distraction. One afternoon, I guess I didn't shut it right because he walked up to me as I was sitting there on the floor. He put his head up against my shoulder, and I could hear very clearly a voice say, "Mom, I am SO tired!"

Wow! I went to my computer and searched "how can you tell if your dog is in pain?" A page popped up from the website of a vet with exactly that title: *How Can You Tell If Your Dog Is In Pain?* It said a dog will not let you know he is in pain until it is really bad. He will lick himself a lot and pant all the time even if it is not hot. He will walk around in circles and his tail will be between his legs. All of these things were going on with Bud. He would go out in the back yard and walk in circles, even if the sprinklers were on. His claws were clinched, his tail was between his legs, he panted a lot, he licked his paws all the time.

I told him if he really loved me, he would have a heart attack like Zildjian did! Reluctantly, I made the appointment to take him in. It was set for the next Monday afternoon, which meant I had to live through the weekend with this hanging over me. I made the decision to stay totally focused on what I was doing in each moment and not on taking him in. On that Monday, I volunteered at the Red Cross office and said to myself, "Right now, I am working at the Red Cross." Then I said, "Right now, I am eating lunch." Then I said, "Right now, I am driving home." Then I said, "Right now, I am putting him in the car. Right now, I am waiting for the doctor to take care of three emergencies and *now* I am taking him in to be put down." I was able to stay in the present moment and keep the fear out of my mind until it came to the actual moment of putting him on the table.

I really surprised myself that I was actually able to do it. But I realized it was perfectly OK to break down and cry at the vet's office and let her give me a big, loving hug, as she cried too. It was fascinating to be there, petting him and then feeling the stark contrast after he passed on. I understood the phrase "dead weight." After his life force left his body, his skin became almost solid, no fluidity left. What an amazing process!

<hr />

BOTTOM LINE: Since I have always had a fear about taking a pet in to be put to sleep, GUDSSATI set it up so I would get the opportunity to experience it and let go of it.

LET GO OF THAT JUSTIFIED OUTRAGE!

You have no idea of the tremendous release and deep peace that comes from meeting yourself and your brothers totally without judgment.

- A Course in Miracles

We hear a lot about forgiveness now, and everyone is saying basically the same thing, so it is easy to just turn it off.

If you are holding on to something someone said or did to you, stop and ask yourself if it is really serving *you* to be so adamant and determined you refuse to forgive that person. Look at all the power you are giving to him or her. *You* are still boiling about it and the other person has probably forgotten all about it years ago. She is sleeping soundly and you are the one who is still replaying the incident to be sure to keep it alive.

Don't forget my story about Ho'Oponopono. That person volunteered to come into your life to help you learn to forgive. She is willing to absorb all of your attack arrows because she (on a soul level) truly loves you and wants you to grow and learn.

Think of all the stories of people who were almost killed by someone who ended up getting to know the bad guy and learning to release any resentment against him. We have a friend who shot down an enemy pilot during the Vietnamese war, and he made a very concerted effort to find that pilot to express his sorrow that he had attacked and almost killed him because of some absurd disagreement between our governments. They finally did connect and have since become great friends, meeting each other's family and grandchildren, and inviting each other to visit their hometowns and tour their country. The pilot who had been shot down held exactly zero resentment toward our friend for what had happened to him.

Think of how you could tell a much more mature, generous story if you were willing to release your hold on what happened to you so many years ago than to keep holding the emotion of that woundedness in your body. Absolutely it is understandable you were deeply wounded and you feel completely justified in staying in your rage. But is it possible for you to be willing to be the first one to offer peace? If the offense occurred a long time ago, maybe the person who wronged you was very immature and has completely changed by now and would never, ever consider doing the same thing to you today. Look at how much *you* have changed since then!

~∞∞⟨∞∞~

BOTTOM LINE: Any time you are feeling upset or resentment toward someone, remind yourself to *choose peace*. It feels a lot better than choosing anger, sadness, fear, or hate. Do it for *yourself.*

MONEY NOT FLOWING?

Since you have been chosen for this divine assignment, it is essential you allow the abundance of the Universe to flow to you. Get to work knocking down the walls that block this flow.

───◦◦◦◦◦───

Edwene Gaines is a delightful Unity minister from Mentone, Alabama, whose goal is to change the abundance consciousness of the entire planet. She believes that in order to keep abundance flowing in your life, you need to find and get on your purpose, tithe 10% of every bit of money that comes into your life, and forgive *everyone*. I credit her with turning my life around regarding prosperity.

I was a Realtor for 22 years and was fortunate to have a very rewarding career. However, every time I noticed the money was not flowing in, I knew it was because I was not forgiving someone in my life. I would take the time out to sit and focus on who it was and then send loving thoughts to him or her, and I would write it out in my journal. I wrote what the problem was and how I wanted it to change. And soon the money would start flowing again.

Wayne Dyer's Meditation for Manifesting CD is very powerful. It is about 20 minutes and you just sit and make the sound of "ahhh" over and over again. This is the sound of creation and is in the many different names for the Creator: God, Buddha, Krishna, Ra, Allah, etc. I started doing it by saying I wanted "qualified buyers, smooth transactions and fast closings." I did that for just a few days and all of a sudden, we got a cash offer on one of our listings, a contract on some land we had listed, and in just a few weeks, we had 19 contracts in escrow. Finally, I said to my Guides, "OK, I get it. This works. It is OK to back off a little now." I have gone back several times over the years to turn the spigot on again.

Pay attention to what you say about money. Don't ever say you can't afford something; say you are choosing to invest your funds in something else right now. You probably really *do* have the money to buy that one particular item, but if you did, you would be short in other areas of your life. Also, if you find yourself without a job, don't keep telling people you are "unemployed." Keep the energy positive by saying you are "between opportunities." You *are* between opportunities, which can be a very valuable time slot. If you can keep yourself out of fear of the future and *trust* you eventually will find your next job, the time in between can offer you a chance to relax, read, meditate, research possibilities, take a short trip, do some planning. Stay positive—*know* your life is just being re-directed.

BOTTOM LINE: Allow the abundance of the Universe to flow through you in a way that serves the world.

DIARRHEA DOG

My center is balanced and expanding,
pushing resentment, hate and anger
out of my soul.

I have taken a *lot* of classes and workshops over the years and I understand that many times, you could possibly experience a release of emotion, a clearing of negative energy, or a detox. This can manifest in the form of crying, throwing up, getting the "runs," etc. I have an agreement with my Guides that I won't do any throwing up. I am totally OK with crying in front of a crowd of strangers in a class, but an upset stomach is unacceptable.

Ed picked me up at the airport on a beautiful Sunday afternoon when I returned to Phoenix after a week-long workshop and when we stopped at a grocery store on the way home, all of a sudden, I got an attack of the runs! We got to the car and drove home, and I went directly into the bathroom, spending probably two hours in there. I like to call the bathroom the "releasing chamber," because it is symbolic of where you can release a lot of negativity. That night, I just couldn't get out of there! Ed called through the door to ask if I needed anything to help stop it, but I said I didn't because I was releasing a *lot* of emotions. It was important to go through the whole process. I even got in the shower and visualized everything that didn't serve me anymore going down the drain.

I ended up lying on a towel on the floor to just rest. Then our dog Bud came in to check out what was going on with me. As I mentioned before, he was blind and very attached to me. He stepped over me and laid down next to me with my back to him and with his back to the vanity. Then he just started pushing his paws into my back repeatedly until he pretty much pushed me right out of the bathroom. It was like he knew I was done with the releasing, and it was time to get up and get back into life.

I had a chiropractor years ago who said if you start to get sick, you are never coming down with something, you are coming *out* with something.

BOTTOM LINE: Take the time to allow negative energy and toxins to leave your body, no matter what form it takes. Don't take anything to stop it. Let the process take its course as you clear these entities out of your body so you will then be ready to move forward.

I ACTUALLY KEPT MY MOUTH SHUT!

I love you....I honor you...
I know YOU know what's best for you.

When my daughter-in-law was exploring become a Jehovah's Witness, I had a really hard time with it. It felt like all of our family traditions were no longer going to be allowed (or at least she and my son and their kids would not attend any of them). I didn't want to share my opinion, because this was their choice, and if they were guided to the Witnesses, I certainly had no right to talk them out of it. I was the one with the problem and I was the one who needed to change my mind. Once again, I spoke to Hal Lafler, asking him what I should do. He asked what I knew about Jehovah's Witnesses. I said I knew nothing. He suggested I research their beliefs before I made a judgment about it.

I asked my daughter-in-law for some literature on it, and I attended their convention in downtown Phoenix. What I saw there was thousands of very pleasant, happy people—moms, dads, grandmas, babies, little kids. Everyone was helping with the little ones when they got restless by taking turns watching them run around out in the hall. There were actually some of the chosen 144,000 in attendance. I stayed most of one day just to see what it was all about.

I enjoy when the Witnesses come knocking on my door since I have some "experience" with their ideas. I actually read the Watch Tower so I can find places where we agree. What I found is they don't believe in Hell because life here on Earth can sometimes be like living in Hell (common ground there). They are *very* family oriented and have amazing support for each other in the community. When my kids were moving from an apartment to a house, a whole crowd of people came over to help them move (common ground there).

There are also some points where there is not common ground between my beliefs and their beliefs. No need to put any of that in writing here, though. What I concentrated on was finding where we believe the same things. I continued to keep my mouth shut with my son, not saying anything to him that would be taken as criticizing their decision or actions. I wanted to change MY mind, not theirs. Eventually, they made the choice on their own that it no longer served them to continue. I have to admit I was *really* relieved, but I was very proud of myself for staying out of it as much as I could!

BOTTOM LINE: Be willing to let everyone to have his or her own personal point of view, especially if it is different from yours. We can heal the world when we are able to *hear* each other and find common ground.

PAST LIVES??
ARE YOU KIDDING?

It is safe to step into your power at this time. It's about time. Everyone has been waiting for you.

～～∞⧜∞～～

I have no clue whether past lives are true or not, but I have had several experiences during hypnosis where I have become aware of a couple lives that could have influenced this lifetime.

I could see myself walking through some thick woods and coming onto a large "secret" meeting with several hundred people standing there listening to their leader. It was a meeting that for safety reasons had to be held in a remote area out of view of any authority. I felt myself needing to "rescue" them. Eventually, I got the mental message I would not be able to rescue all of them. I needed only to speak to the ones who came up to me and were willing to hear me. The meaning of this life experience was for me to understand I would not be able to help everyone in the world, just the ones I come in contact with.

Several weeks later, I had a session with another practitioner, and she asked me what happened next in that previous vision. I said there was a huge fire. She said, yes, the whole thing happened inside a huge tent and someone set it on fire. She also said I was the speaker! I was not happy about that, but it did symbolize being a leader of many people who were definitely following me and what I was teaching. All of us were burned to death that night.

I also had a memory of a lifetime in Atlantis when I was

the leader of a large temple community. We were there when Atlantis went down. We knew there was *no way* we would be able to be rescued or saved from the coming floods, so we all just calmly sat down and allowed the massive waves to crash over us, taking us all to our deaths in the ocean.

I felt very guilty about the loss of life in both of these instances, but I meditated on it and asked the souls of everyone who died how they felt about it—no one was upset at all. They were all glad to be able to leave the lifetime they had been in, and now they were free to do whatever they want to do. I was able to release the guilt without carrying it in my heart in this lifetime.

I realize now I have had some hesitation about stepping into the role of a leader in my current life because I have had these experiences where everyone who was following me was killed. However, that is exactly why I am in the position I am in now with opening up the Arizona Enlightenment Center. It is important for my soul growth to know people will no longer be killed if they choose to come along with me. Wow!

BOTTOM LINE: Whether past-life experiences really happened or if they are just stories that popped into your mind, they bring ideas that can help you learn so you will be able to better handle the challenges that come up in your current lifetime.

THANK YOU FOR BEING SUCH A PAIN

Every relationship is an assignment.

———❖———

That is the name of a wonderful book by Mark Rosen. It has helped me get past a lot of resentment towards anyone who was causing me some conflict. It has helped me move more into compassion and understanding about why certain negative and frustrating things were happening in my life.

Sometimes, though, it is a lot more satisfying to keep the resentment alive. Sometimes we are just not ready to move on yet. Caroline Myss said in one of her books that the person who you are having such a hard time with is under orders from God to not approve of you so you can grow stronger. Everybody comes into your life to either teach you how to do something or how not to do it. Send each one gratitude for loving you enough to stab you in your heart so you can learn what you signed up to learn.

You may think you are going through pure hell and you can't understand why you have to suffer so much. You stomp your foot at God and say you have had *enough*! When you hit bottom, you are at the most powerful place in your life—because you are ready to make the turn back up to the top, a completely changed person.

Everything that happens in your life happened *for* you, not *to* you. I have an astonishing number of friends who grew up in physically and/or verbally abusive situations. I have always been in awe of them for actually thanking their mother or father or other family member for treating them the way they did because those experiences guided them along their life path so they could become who they are now. They completely understand why it all happened. It allowed them to grow into the strong, spiritually awake person they are today.

Peace of mind comes from not wanting to change others but simply accepting them as they are. True acceptance is always without demands and expectations. See if you can get through just one day with no attack thoughts. Just today. Can you do it?

BOTTOM LINE: You are not a victim. You are a volunteer. Learn from your experiences so you can help others get through similar situations.

EVEN SPORTS CAN
BE SPIRITUAL

*Watching an example of good sportsmanship fills
us with an appreciation for the love and kindness
that dwells in people all over the world.*

~~~❦~~~

My mother was a sports fanatic. She loved NBA, NFL
and baseball. She knew all the stats, the players, the coach-
es. We grew up with the sound of baseball games on the
radio. Unfortunately, Ed and I had zero interest in any kind
of sports. We would walk into her house and start talking,
even though the Suns were tied with only 30 seconds left.
This was back before there was anything that could have
recorded it so she could watch it later.

Mom died in 1990 and shortly after that, Charles Barkley
came to the Suns, and they went all the way to the NBA
finals against the Chicago Bulls. The entire state of Arizona
got hooked on the playoffs, and I got hooked on basketball. Too bad I never was able to talk with Mom about the
games. I don't know what kind of fan she was: die-hard or
fair-weather.

I recently realized most of my spiritual friends have no
interest in sports. They really don't know what is going on
with the teams. They don't even know who Steve Nash is. I
think the main problem is the competition. They aren't in to
watching one team try to annihilate the other team. I have
to agree I don't like that either. My favorite kind of game
is one where the score is really close, each team is playing
awesome basketball, and it is too bad one team has to lose

since they are both so good.

However, I also have noticed there really are a few times when a sports event can exhibit some very spiritual qualities. One is when the "wave" gets started spontaneously in one part of the arena. It takes several attempts to get going, but after a few minutes, almost everyone joins in the fun. That is a great demonstration of oneness. Another time is when the star player gets hurt and has to go to the locker room right when the game is really close. The game goes on with everyone totally involved. All of a sudden, the star returns from the locker room and a huge roar ensues. How does that happen? Everybody is not sitting there staring at the tunnel that leads to the locker room, but it is amazing how fast the crowd connects at the sight of their hero returning to the game. Yet another example is when a fan gets an opportunity to make a shot from mid court and a chance to win a truck or $77,777. If he makes it, the whole arena of fans erupts in total happiness for him—a complete stranger. At that moment, everyone comes together.

BOTTOM LINE: It does not matter if the person next to you at the game is Republican or Democrat or born-again Christian or Muslim or Atheist. We all connect as human beings.

I HAVE LOST MY DEBIT CARD AGAIN!

*You have an internal assistant available
to you at every moment.*

~~~⚜~~~

For some reason, I have been misplacing my debit card, my driver's license, my keys, and various other personal items. It is so frustrating to see how much time I waste trying to find stuff.

I took a Certification Course in "Dream Yoga," a modality to help people interpret the symbolism in their dreams, and in one of my own dreams, I dropped my keys into a hole in the bed of a pickup truck. In Dream Yoga, we interview the characters in the dream—specifically the inanimate objects—to see what message they have for the dreamer. When I went through the process of interviewing the hole in the truck, the message to me was that when I drop the keys in that hole, it is a subconscious delay tactic, keeping me from moving forward.

I see this also applies to my current life when I misplace my keys or driver's license. For some reason, I am holding myself back from stepping into my true destiny—perhaps because my "assignment" seems so huge and overwhelming.

Recently, I have remembered to ask my Guides. I had lost my driver's license AGAIN, so I said, "OK, Guides, help me find my license. I know YOU know where it is." The next day, I got a call from the bank saying I had left it at their branch. The week after that, I couldn't find my keys, and again I said, "OK, Guides, help me find my keys.

I know YOU know where they are." Then my neighbor called to say she had found them in her car from when she drove us to our yoga class.

I was really pleased to see how fast I was able to find them. I know I will remember sooner now to ask when I lose something else.

For years, Ed and I have known to ask our Guides to help us find something. You have probably done that, too, without even knowing it. We would look all over the house and say, "OK, Guides, where is it?" Pretty soon we would "get the thought" to look in the bottom drawer in the dresser, and there it would be.

BOTTOM LINE: Isn't it fascinating
you ALWAYS find what you are looking
for in the LAST place you look?!

SOMETHING TOLD US SOMETHING WAS WRONG

Everyone is profoundly clairvoyant.
Your gifts are needed in the world NOW.

Ed has always seemed to be intuitively connected with our kids. Dan was very trustworthy about being home on time at night, and we never worried about what he was doing or that he was up to something. He could come home at 3:00 in the morning and we knew it was no big deal. He didn't drink or smoke or use drugs, and he could be everybody's designated driver.

One night when he was in high school, he went out with a friend and we expected him to be home by 11:00. Ed and I were getting ready to go to bed and he was worried we had not heard from him. He started pacing around and did what every good parent would do—go outside and look up and down the street. That was sure to bring him right home. He came back in and was standing next to the phone when it rang. It was the father of Dan's friend, calling to tell us there had been an accident and Dan was at the hospital. We rushed over to the ER and found him laying on a gurney, waiting to get stitches in his lip. He had gone through the windshield and his face looked like hamburger. Going through a windshield is not necessarily bad; it is the coming back through that does the damage as your face scrapes against all the broken glass.

What was it that made Ed know something had happened to Dan?

Pay attention to the times in your life when you intuitively connect with a friend or family member. You may think it is just a coincidence, but you are just not recognizing this is your intuition. Our job is to learn to follow the guidance of our gut feelings. These feelings are usually the best advice we will get. Many times people ignore their inner instructions and end up suffering in some way for not trusting them.

BOTTOM LINE: We ALL have the "gift."
We ALL get gut feelings about something or someone.

TAKE THE HASSLE
OUT OF CHRISTMAS

"Our life is frittered away by detail.
Simplify. Simplify. Simplify."

- Henry David Thoreau

Christmas used to be a major event for me that included a huge dose of stress. I would buy seven presents for each kid in the family plus four for Ed. I realized that since I am not very demonstrative about *speaking* that I love them, I could show it buy buying stuff for them! I felt that four would not be enough, five or six would be acceptable, but seven was definitely enough—eight was over the top.

One year, *both* of our kids came to me and said they really didn't need all that stuff. One son's inlaws also gave that many, so they would exit Christmas with a truckload full of little and big additions to their home; and the other son's inlaws would draw names and each person would get one or two gifts. This was a major shift for me, but I must admit I LOVE it. It has taken 75% of the stress out of the Christmas season, and I would have *never* made that suggestion to them. This meant I eliminated the need to purchase *thirty-two* presents!!! Woo Hoo! (Sorry I was no longer contributing to a healthy economy by spending more during the holiday season!)

I do have to admit, though, I really miss filling the stockings. I had such fun searching out a whole bunch of very cool little things for each person. That tradition was sort of easy to let go of since it would cost a small fortune to fill up the relatively large stockings we had for each person.

We also released the kids from having to buy us presents for Mother's Day, Father's Day, birthdays, anniversaries, and so on. I know it is really hard to find something special for someone who just goes out and buys it if something comes up she would like. So they can let go of that obligation. Can you imagine how freeing it would feel to you to not have to buy gifts for a long list of family and friends?

Since 2003, we have hosted a potluck lunch on Christmas Day for a bunch of our friends who don't have other family to be with that day. Since everyone brings the food, all I have to do is set up the tables and organize the kitchen to display all the goodies. Even though we are having about 30 people over for lunch, it is a relatively un-stressful event and we love doing it. We have formed a lovely spiritual family gathering at these potlucks every year, and we also have time to spend with our own family later that day.

BOTTOM LINE: Pay attention to the unnecessary routines and self-imposed deadlines you pile on your own back every day and see what you can eliminate to make your life flow so much smoother.

YOU CAN'T
UNLEARN THAT

If you are not green and growing,
you are ripe and rotting.

Have you noticed that when you see something you have never seen before, you run it through every experience and bit of knowledge you have stored in your mind to explain it? When you see an airplane in the daytime sky, you don't freak out about what the heck it is because you have seen hundreds of them before. If you can't find something in your memory to explain it, then you start to get a little nervous since this is something new, something unexplainable.

I went into a store last year and for the first time I saw brussel sprouts still attached to the stalk they grow on. I had *no* clue that is how they grow. But after I saw that, I can never "un-know" it. I had expanded my consciousness.

We visited some friends in Colorado several years ago and when it was time for dinner, Claudette went out to their garden and picked some asparagus. I had never even thought about how asparagus grows. Another awesome revelation!

In our city, we have trash cans built into the ground so we don't have the unsightly line of garbage containers lined up down every street on trash pickup day. Recently, during a class at our house, the garbage truck came by to collect the trash. Isela, the facilitator of the class, had never seen such a thing: inground trash cans! She was totally amazed, and now she can never un-learn that.

GUDSSATI is similar to that. We are all expressions of

God, even the bad guys like mass murderers, child molesters, rapists. We are all here on the planet having experiences and sending information back to the Creator. When that happens, the consciousness of All That Is expands, which is absolutely necessary to keep everything in constant motion and growing.

BOTTOM LINE: It is essential for us to keep growing while we are on the planet, just like it is essential for GUDSSATI to keep growing and expanding.

IN THIS MOMENT, YOU HAVE EVERYTHING YOU NEED

*"My world is perfectly protected
and perfectly united..."*

- A Course in Miracles

~~~oooioooo~~~

It's interesting how so many people spend (invest?) so much of their time (life force energy?) in worrying. They think they have to constantly be doing *something* to ensure their future will be comfortable and secure.

Lost Horizon is a famous book and movie about a group of British travelers whose plane crashes high in the snowy mountains of Tibet, and they are rescued by friendly people from a local village. It turns out this "village" is really Shangri-la/Heaven/Utopia, where everything is lovely, beautiful, peaceful, safe, and abundant. The head monk spends a lot of time sharing the philosophy of the village with Conway, the leader of the British group. This is one of the statements in the book that really affected me: "There is no need for banks in Shangri-la because there is no uncertain future to plan for." What a concept!! Total trust you will have everything you need when you need it. No need to save up for anything.

Several times I have gone to some presentation or class and bought the latest gadget only to come home and find we *already* have one of those! This is one more reminder that we actually have *everything* we need!

Look around you and see that in this moment, you do

have everything you need—a place to live, a car or some other way to get wherever you need to go, food in the cupboard, indoor plumbing, air conditioning and heating, a bed to sleep on, a table and chair, running water, air to breathe. You are blessed and you are always taken care of. So sit back and watch for the next great adventure life has planned for you.

BOTTOM LINE: *You are held in the arms of the Father and you are completely safe.*

YOU ARE AN INFINITE BEING

No one has been falsely chosen. Let go of any self doubt that is holding you back. You are here in this dream by choice. Do you have any idea of what you bring to the planet?

Most of our problems in life come up because we allow our human-ness to take charge. We get our feelings hurt, we feel unworthy, we feel guilty about some little thing we did or said, we feel jealous of somebody. The problem is you forget *WHO you really are*. We are Infinite Beings, playing a role in a human play. Every time you get upset, see how fast you can remember *WHO you really are* so you can quickly shift back into peace, calm, and confidence.

I heard Deepak Chopra once tell the story about being with his granddaughter out in the countryside in total darkness where there were no artificial lights. They looked up at the stars and he pointed one out to her saying the light left that star millions of years ago and is focused here on the planet at this time. He told her *we* are basically Light that left a star system millions of years ago and that Light is focused at this time as *us*. We have come from a faraway place and chose to focus our Light here on the planet at *this* time for a very specific purpose. *That* is *WHO we really are*, and if we can remember that, it is easy to shift out of any human-based funk and back into our power and strength.

Do you think you are blocked or somehow defective if you can't feel the energy of a crystal that is supposed to be so powerful? Well, what if you don't feel it because you are *already* at that level of vibration? Hmmmm.

A friend of mine described some guidance he got when he was attending a spiritual conference. It was the third day of sessions and he decided to go back to his room to take a short nap. After a while, he got a very strong message he needed to get back downstairs. He got up and went back to the conference session. He waited and waited, expecting something to happen that would possibly change his life since his Guides told him to get back to the room. Nothing happened and he got a little impatient. He asked his Guides what the heck was up and he heard, "Why do you think you need to be in the room so someone can say something that will affect you? Why can't you believe maybe someone else needs to hear something from *you*? Maybe the room needs *your* Light." What a concept!

<hr>

BOTTOM LINE: God has *your* picture on His dresser!

ARE YOU READY
TO GET ON WITH IT?

*"We are here at this time to hold the Light
for those who do not yet have the Light."*

\- Norma Lynne Ormandy

Mike Quinsey tells a story on one of his DVD programs about a family of ducks. When it is time, the mother duck leaves the area of the water to find a safe place to lay her eggs. After they all hatch, it is time to lead them to the water. She does not wait to "get her ducks in a row," she just starts out toward the water (her goal) and all the ducklings fall in place behind her, heading out to their next new experience: finding out they already *know* how to swim.

*Do you really think you will be thrown out there to get on stage or in front of people and not have the ability to get the message across? You already know what to say! You know what to do! Just get on with it and have total faith to know your Guides will be there with you! Why would they guide you to this point and not support you when you agree to step out in faith? They will be there with you!

You keep thinking what you are doing isn't really your true purpose because it looks too easy, too comfortable. That's because that is *what you are supposed to do. You are already doing your purpose and as you grow, your purpose will shift into another level.*

You think sometimes your prayers aren't answered, yet your prayers have *been answered. You just haven't ac-*

cepted the answer—and don't forget, sometimes the answer is no.

When you feel like nothing is happening to move you forward into your divine purpose, just think of a butterfly in a cocoon. If you observe the cocoon from the outside, it looks like absolutely nothing is happening. Yet, a miraculous, total transformation is taking place, and when the time is RIGHT, a butterfly emerges in all its glory.

Look around at what you have been guided to do in life. You are being groomed for your life purpose. You may not recognize the next level. You will be guided to that new version as well.

<hr/>

BOTTOM LINE: You have had the seeds of greatness planted inside you. All your experiences have been fertilizing them, so when it is time, they will blossom effortlessly as your inner wisdom awakens.

CONCLUSION

I have been writing this book my whole life and I didn't even know it. As I look back, I can see every experience I went through expanded my consciousness and got added to my collection of stories. It's funny to think I spent so much time asking what I was supposed to be doing in life, and I had no clue I was already *doing* it.

For some reason, I felt an urgency to get this book done. I got message after message to "write the book." When I finally sat down to get started on it, the stories just flowed out onto the paper. It has been so much fun, and I can't wait to get going on Volume 2. New stories are already coming in.

I have, however, gotten quite irritated to be interrupted by people who are doing the same thing I am. Just recently, my friend Trish told me she heard about someone who wrote a book just like mine with a lot of short stories. My first reaction was to be upset, but then my Guides reminded me someone may need to hear an idea 17 times before he really *gets* it, and I need to be willing to be #15. Everyone writing books, songs, movies, or giving seminars is saying the same thing but putting a different perspective on it. A student will finally *hear* it when he finds a teacher who speaks his language.

I hope you have enjoyed the book as much as I have enjoyed writing it. Pass it on to everyone you know. (We can always think of a family member or friend who *needs* to read it. Certainly *we* didn't really need it.!)

We invite you to order the *You Already Know This—Guidebook* to start your journey to remembering you have inner guidance and learning how to connect with it. It is available at www.OriginalInspirationPublishing.com. Are you ready?

ABOUT THE AUTHOR

Heather M. Clarke has a passion for helping other people discover their own spirituality and enlightenment. In 2005, she started with a dream in a little house—the Arizona Enlightenment Center. It has since grown to an ever-bigger family with a vision for the future as they create a community, locally and globally, to touch people and help them embrace their own greatness.

She graduated Arizona State University in 1967 with a Bachelors Degree in Business Administration. She also attended the Southwest Institute of Healing Arts, achieving certifications in Spiritual Studies and Dream Interpretation. She spent over twenty years as a residential real estate agent, helping many young families purchase their first home.

She devoted four years to serving as a Red Cross volunteer, assisting families who were affected by major disasters such as fires, floods, or storms. She also served at the Red Cross Headquarters in Falls Church, Virginia, and in New York City during the 9/11 response.

Heather is the Founder and Executive Director of the Arizona Enlightenment Center, coordinating events, gathering the team, and holding the vision for the upcoming manifestation of the Center. She has attended a vast array of workshops and seminars and studied with the leading spiritual minds of the day. This has given her the ability to be an effective resource—a messenger—for others, by having gained experience and knowledge from a wide assortment of teachers, healers, gurus, authors, and from ordinary people who have affected her life in extraordinary ways. She feels the Arizona Enlightenment Center is her purpose, and she devotes her life to gathering people into a thriving spiritual community.

www.ingramcontent.com/pod-product-compliance
Lightning Source LLC
Chambersburg PA
CBHW060818050426
42449CB00008B/1717